Mr. T and Mr. B

B for BEACH

Written and Illustrated by

Lucinda Marks

Mr. T and Mr. B
Written and illustrated by Lucinda Marks
Copyright 2019, All Rights Reserved
ISBN 978-1-947844-85-8
Published by Suzeteo Enterprises

For Tanner

You were the first to call me Grandma.

Thank you for bringing such joy to my heart!

Life is never boring when you are around.

Keep spreading joy wherever you go.

Love you now and always!

Meet Mr. T, he is nice and funny.
Meet his best friend, a little black bunny.

Mr. T

Mr. B

What an adventure it will be
Searching for words with T or B.

BOOK

BOAT

TUBA

TOY

TURKEY

TRAIN

Mr. T is ready. It is time to go.
Mr. B grabs a snack and a cappuccino.

Mr. T's adventure begins on the train
Traveling the scenic rocky terrain.

Mr. B backpacks to his little brown boat
Buoyantly bobbing and staying afloat.

Mr. T takes his towel on a tropical trip,
Gentle tides for snorkeling, time for a dip.

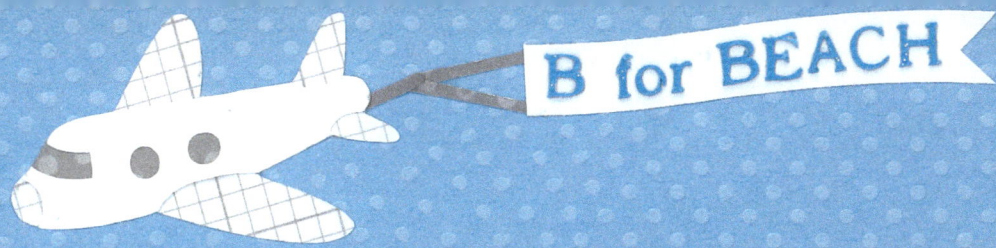

Mr. B loves the beach with waves and sand
Balancing his body as he raises his hand.

Mr. T has his favorite three toys,
A T-rex, a tractor, a truck that makes a noise.

Mr. B buries his nose in a book
About four little children and the walk they took.

FOUR
LITTLE
CHILDREN

Lucinda M.

Mr. T follows the trail to camp.
His tent is terrific. It never gets damp.

Mr. B visits goats at the farm.
Bobby and Billy live in the barn.

Mr. T sees a turkey, friendly and tame.
He tosses a taco and says, "What's your name?"

THOMAS

Mr. B sees a buffalo, bashful and shy.
He brings it ice cream and blueberry pie.

Mr. T takes his telescope to find a star pattern.
He tilts it again to find Venus and Saturn.

Mr. B points up to the dark blue sky.
The Big Dipper is glowing way up high.

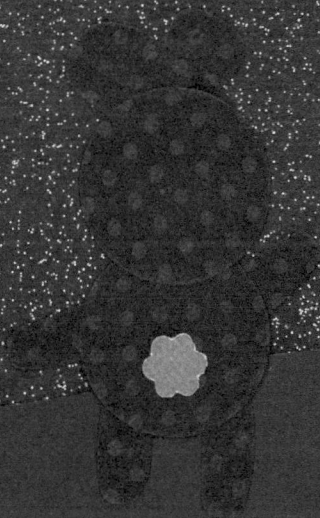

Mr. T toots his tubby tubular tuba.
He plays a tune that goes duba duba duba.

Mr. B brings along his big baritone bass.
The ballad keeps up with the tuba duba pace.

Mr. T is tired, ready to relax.
Time to get moving, make some tracks.
Mr. B bounces down the bumpy path,
Ready for a snack and a bubble bath.

Grandma has the picnic table ready and set,
Food that starts with T and B, from the alphabet ...
Toast, and tangerines, with tortilla chips,
Bananas, blackberries, butterscotch whips.

Your turn now to find what was missed,
Go back in the book, find this list.

T

Turtle
Toad
Tree
Trumpet
Tern
Tulip

B

Binoculars
Butterfly
Boogie Board
Bobber
Balloon
Baby Bird Ballerina

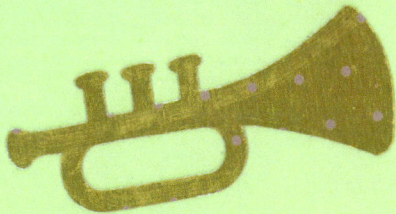

Tongue Twister Sentences

Mr. T travels on the train through a tremendously tall mountain terrain.
Mr. B bobs his bobber while fishing in his brown buoyant bass boat.

Mr. T totes turquoise swimming trunks and a towel for his tropical trip.
Mr. B balances his body on a boogie board at the beach.

Mr. T transports the toy tractor and the toy truck to the tiny track.
Mr. B reads a book as he begins to drink his berry juice being careful not to belch.

Mr. T treks up the trail to set up his red and tan tent under a Tamarack tree.
Mr. B buys bananas for the two bleating goats named Billy and Bobby.

Mr. T tastes tacos on Tuesday with a tame turkey named Thomas.
Mr. B wants to borrow binoculars to watch butterflies bounce in the breeze.

Mr. T takes the telescope and turns it toward the twinkling sky at twilight.
Mr. B points to the brilliantly beautiful Big Dipper.

Mr. T totes his tubby tuba and toots twelve tunes for two toads.
Mr. B bellows out a ballad while playing his bass as a baby bird does ballet.

Mr. T tastes tangerines, toast, and tortilla chips trying not to talk with his mouth full.
Mr. B eats bits of bananas, blackberries, and butterscotch whips before his bubble bath.

www.ingramcontent.com/pod-product-compliance
Lightning Source LLC
Chambersburg PA
CBHW040453100426

42813CB00022BA/2988